MW01065120

# You &
# Others

**Adapted From Material Written By**

**Gina Anderson • Exie Barber**
**John R. Hembree • John Maempa**

**Radiant Life**
1445 Boonville Avenue
Springfield, Missouri 65802–1894
02-0151

National Director: Arlyn R. Pember
Editor in Chief: Michael H. Clarensau
Adult Editor: Paul W. Smith
Series Coordinator: Aaron D. Morgan
Design/Cover Illustration: Jared Van Bruaene

Copyright © 1999 Gospel Publishing House
1445 Boonville Avenue, Springfield, Missouri 65802–1894

All rights reserved. No part of this book may be reproduced in any form without permission in writing from the publisher, except in the case of brief quotations embodied in critical articles or reviews.

All Scripture quotations, unless noted otherwise, are from the Holy Bible, New International Version. Copyright © 1973, 1978, 1984, International Bible Society. Used by permission of Zondervan Bible Publishers.

Printed in the United States of America

ISBN 0–88243–151–X

The leader guide for this book can be ordered from Gospel Publishing House (02–0251) at 1–800–641–4310.

# Contents

# Preface

*You & Others*, one of four books in the *Biblical Living Series*, will lead you in developing healthy relationships with others, strengthening those relationships with godly and mutually beneficial communication, and gaining a heart to serve and win others to Christ. Each chapter will help you evaluate relevant Bible passages by asking you thought-provoking questions, many of which call on you to make application to your personal life.

You can read *You & Others* on its own or as a part of the *Biblical Living Series*. It is recommended you read only one chapter a week so you can allow each chapter's biblical truths and instructions time to "sink in." Some of the questions will require ongoing action on your part; do not neglect these if you want to get the full benefit from this book.

If you are reading *You & Others* as part of a small group or a Sunday School class, be sure to complete the assigned chapter before each meeting. The discussions, work sheets, and activities in which you will participate during your group's next meeting will be most beneficial if you have read and filled out the chapter being covered.

This preface would not be complete without recognizing the authors whose studies for Radiant Life's young adult and adult dated curriculum were adapted for this book. Gina Anderson is a pastor's wife and a freelance writer. John Maempa is the general editor of Assemblies of God foreign missions publications. John R. Hembree is associate pastor of discipleship in a local congregation. And Exie Barber pastors a church.

Aaron Morgan
*Biblical Living Series* Coordinator
Springfield, Missouri

# Part One

# Building Relationships

In heaven, believers from all places and times will enjoy eternity with God, worshiping and communing with Him together. While heaven will be more joyous than you can imagine, there is one hint of its joy that is available to you today—Christian friendships. The bonds established between believers in this life point ahead to the love that will be shared in the body of Christ forever.

Christian friendships also offer support during the trials of this life and the world's hostility. Where unsaved friends may challenge your public testimony, a trusted believing friend can encourage your faith to grow. Instead of calling on you to compromise your godly standards, your Christian friends can help you remain committed to righteousness.

Friendship, of course, requires effort on your part. The next three chapters, besides pointing out the blessings enjoyed through Christian friendships, will remind you of the steps you must take in order to build such relationships.

**Godly friendships can influence you toward what is good.**

# Developing Friendships

Friendship is a powerful force. If established on a godly foundation, it can give you strength and encouragement; if misdirected, it can bring your life to ruin. Unfortunately, the need for friendship is so great that many people enter it with little thought about the long-term consequences of who their friends are. Many young people join gangs, for instance, not for the appeal of violence or narcotics, but to gain a tight-knit group of friends; they simply want to belong.

If Satan can use the desire for friendship to draw people into evil, how much more can Jesus work in you to develop friendships which influence you to live a godly life. You must recognize the impact godly friendships can have on your walk with God and how much unconditional love, unwavering commitment, and unfailing encouragement can benefit those whom you call friends.

## Being Friendly

Being a friendly person is the first step toward creating wonderful friendships. The most natural place for this is in the church. It is easy to exhibit friendliness to others in your church because they are family, your brothers and sisters in Christ. Because of this family tie, your Christian friendships have the potential to be that much closer than your other relationships. Proverbs 17:17 reflects the potential of a friendship between fellow believers: "A friend loves at all times, and a brother is born for adversity."

**1–1.** *How do your relationships with other believers differ from those you have with unsaved people?*

With the rise of large churches and this society's general mobility, it is vital that you remember that friendships among believers are never supposed to be loosely knit or casually maintained. You have likely encountered Christians who claimed to be your friends, yet whose commitment to you did not extend beyond surface congeniality. You are true siblings through Christ, and your desire to be friendly must be based on that bond of family.

**1–2.** *What warning does Proverbs 18:24 issue about casual friendships? (Read this verse in a modern translation.)*

This does not mean you are only to be a friend to other believers. Job 29:11–17 outlines your responsibility to stretch yourself by freely offering your friendship and support regardless of a person's station in life. Job was known for his assistance to those in poverty and personal distress (verses 11–13). He was an honest and just friend, who served others out of a deep sense of God's righteousness, not just out of a desire to be charitable (verse 14). The physical limitations of others did not cause him to shrink back from being a friend, nor did economic poverty or ethnic differences (verses 15,16). He was also not afraid to stand up for those too weak to overcome evil or injustice on their own (verse 17).

Your church, neighborhood, and city are filled with people who fit the descriptions of those mentioned in Job 29. You may be tempted to avoid contact with these groups, because you fear that the friendships will be one-sided or will not benefit you. However, a beneficial friendship is one that God uses to develop greater character in you. Purposing to be friendly in spite of social, economic, or cultural differences allows God to use you for greater good. Your commitment to show the love of Christ can prepare needy hearts to receive the gospel.

1–3. *Name an unbeliever with whom you have been less than friendly because you saw no potential benefit from having a relationship with him or her. What can you do to take the first step in building a friendship?*

# Avoiding Threats To Friendship

Some friendships remain close for many years; others gradually drift apart. Sadly, still others are divided by careless words, misused possessions, or broken trust.

An unguarded tongue has destroyed many friendships. If you deliberately speak ill of another person, such words are sure to cause division (Proverbs 16:28). God's will is to promote love, not discord. Your model is Jesus, the perfect example of One who overlooks your many faults to meet your needs (17:9). You must allow the Spirit to search your heart for your true motives, and pray earnestly that God will teach you to weigh your words before you speak.

**1–4.** *How have hurtful words seriously damaged one of your friendships? How were you able to mend it?*

Money is another potential divider of friends, particularly when one friend prospers financially and the other does not. While you must always be willing to help a friend in need, the Bible speaks strongly against providing security for another's financial indebtedness (Proverbs 17:18; 6:1–5). You will not deepen your friendship with the borrower by the transaction, and there is great potential for destroying the friendship if he or she does not repay the loan. Giving, not loaning or co-signing for a loan, seems to be the scriptural way to handle financial transactions between friends.

1–5. *Have you had a friendship strained over monetary issues? What was the long-term impact on your friendship?*

The most devastating blow to a friendship is betrayal. Jesus himself suffered this blow. Judas used his knowledge of the Lord's activities to lead an armed party to the Garden of Gethsemane (Matthew 26:47). He used the kiss, a gesture of friendship, as his betraying signal (verses 48,49). And when his gentlest and most devoted Friend was arrested, he looked on with approval (verse 50).

No one knows exactly why Judas betrayed the Lord, but you see in Jesus' response a willingness to forgive him, just as He has forgiven you. Judas was too overcome with remorse to accept that forgiveness, but it was available. If you want to remain in right standing with God, you must also extend the gift of forgiveness to the friends who have betrayed you.

1–6. *Think of a former friend with whom you broke ties because he or she betrayed your trust. What do you need to do to forgive this person and take the first step toward reconciliation?*

# Building Up Each Other

The best way to preserve a friendship is to edify the other person, building him or her up by "speaking the truth in love" (Ephesians 4:15). To preserve honesty in a friendship, you must be willing to correct friends whose actions or words are potentially destructive (Proverbs 27:5,6). You must also be willing to receive correction so your friendships remain open and free of misunderstanding.

1–7.   *Do you think it is easy or difficult to correct close friends? What about accepting correction from them? Explain your answers.*

Edifying others also involves giving wise counsel. Perhaps your best counsel is a listening ear. As friends share worries and heartaches, your sympathetic presence is soothing to their wounded spirits (27:9). Your encouraging counsel can refresh and restore the friend whose joy has ebbed away.

1–8.   *Write about a time you were blessed by the listening ear of a good friend. What did this mean to you?*

Another aspect of building up others is befriending the hurting. When disaster strikes, those close to one another often bind together in ways they never have before (verse 10). In order to build others up and strengthen your friendships, you must be aware of these opportunities.

God can use faithful, godly friends to point out weak areas in your spiritual walk. Proverbs 27:17 uses the illustration of iron sharpening iron to show the character-forming potential of a godly friendship. Each friend influences the other.

You must also encourage others by being compassionate and understanding when your friends are weak in spiritual matters (Romans 15:1,2). This does not mean you need to compromise your integrity. Rather, you must consider the feelings of others before your own. Your human nature makes you susceptible to an attitude of superiority, but placing the edification of others before your own need to be built up is a guard against these attitudes and a blessing to the body of Christ (1 Thessalonians 5:11).

**1–9.** *Is it necessary to put others before yourself to build them up? Why or why not?*

# Chapter Review

Every believer is part of the Church, with a responsibility for ministry. One of your greatest responsibilities is to build godly friendships. A solid spiritual friendship is one wherein both people are willing to maintain the relationship through specific acts of the will. Sometimes you will not feel friendly, nor will your friends always meet your expectations. At times, your old nature will want to tear others down, rather than build them up.

*1–10.  How have you experienced the need to be a friend when you did not feel like being one? What came of your being friendly despite your feelings?*

Jesus taught that any act performed for another believer is an action received by Him and reckoned as done for Him. This means you are committed by an even higher loyalty than friendship itself to be friendly in all situations, to avoid actions and attitudes that can divide friends, and to encourage your friends toward greater godliness. Such commitment arises from a desire to conform your will to God's will, despite how your thoughts, emotions, or old nature may oppose you. The result will be friends who are influenced toward good. What kind of friendships are you building?

Godly friends love and support one another in every circumstance.

2

# Sticking With Each Other

Put yourself in the place of Jill. For the third evening in a row, the telephone rings during dinner. It is Barbara, who has also dropped by the house twice this week. Barbara has many problems, and she needs a godly friend. Only Jesus can change her circumstances, but if Jill does not minister His love to her, who will?

The Lord has called you to be a godly friend in a world that is often unfriendly. He has commanded you to share the love He has so bountifully bestowed on you. Lonely people fill homes, cities, small communities, and even churches. Through the examples of Scripture, the greatest Friend can teach you what godly friendship truly means.

## Providing Companionship

A major responsibility of a godly friend is to be a consistent companion. A companion is one who helps another in life's labor—a coworker sharing a common goal. As a genuine companion, you can give your friends aid in times of distress, security against the world's buffeting, and strength during testing (see Ecclesiastes 4:9–12). You must be willing to empathize with the feelings and sorrows of your friends, and if possible, act to alleviate these trials.

The events of the night before Christ's crucifixion poignantly reveal that even Jesus needed and desired this type of companionship. In the midnight hour of His soul, He hoped to share His burden with those closest to Him (Matthew 26:36–40). Sadly, the disciples found themselves physically and emotionally depleted from recent events. Although Jesus continually displayed concern for them (verse 41), the disciples seemed unable to provide strength and encouragement for their dearest Friend.

2–1.    Have you found yourself in a situation similar to that of the disciples? Did you put aside your wants to provide the encouragement your friend needed? What happened?

When you are exhausted, hurting, or in need yourself, you may not a think you have the emotional stamina to be a good companion. However, the realization of your own needs should not make you less willing to provide compassionate companionship, but more so. The Spirit of God can give you the ability to extend the gentle hand, provide the listening ear, or speak the soothing words of a godly companion. As you are obedient, the Holy Spirit will minister through you in ways you could never have hoped to minister in your own strength.

2–2.   *How do you think the Holy Spirit can help you be a better companion to those who need one?*

Since creation, companionship has been a genuine human need. In sharp contrast to Christ's garden of sorrow, the first man was placed in a garden of joy. Yet Adam found himself without a companion. God declared this condition unsuitable (Genesis 2:18), and created a unique helper from Adam's side (verses 21,22). Eve provided the human warmth and security Adam craved (verse 20).

The Book of Ruth give another example of companionship. Naomi had faced grief, setbacks, and spiritual and emotional famine. In her distress, God blessed her with the devoted companionship of her daughter-in-law, Ruth. The previous years had been difficult for the women; neither knew what waited for them in Bethlehem. Yet Ruth chose to trust God and to remain faithful to Naomi (Ruth 1:16–18).

2–3.   *Which example of companionship—Eve or Ruth—means the most to you? Why do you think this is?*

Like Ruth, you have a choice. When a friend is in the middle of uncertain circumstances, it is imperative that you choose to provide the loving companionship he or she needs. God will use the support of Christian friends to enable His children to persevere in faith and overcome adversity.

**2–4.** *List three people you know are in need of companionship at this moment. Select one of them and record what you choose to do this week to be there for this person.*

# Communicating Love

Of equal importance in good friendships is being able to communicate love, as the Old Testament story of David and Jonathan exemplifies (1 Samuel 18:1–4). Jonathan cared greatly about David and showed it with his actions (verse 1). The friends made a covenant of their dedication to one another and the will to make their friendship a lasting one.

Jonathan understood that love must be a sacrifice. He stripped himself of his princely robe and surrendered all weapons of war (verse 4). Jonathan made himself vulnerable to David. There was no room for pretentiousness in this friendship, no place for defensive armor to keep the other person at a distance. In order to communicate biblical love, you too must be willing to be vulnerable, giving up your facade in order to let others know you deeply.

2–5.  Modern friendships are rarely as deep and vulnerable as that between David and Jonathan, nor do many friends share a genuine, brotherly love. Why do you think this is so?

The love communicated in your friendships must spring from your deep and lasting love for the Lord. Because your life has been transformed by the eternal truth of God's Word, you can love your friends with a purity and fervency unequaled in worldly relationships (1 Peter 1:22). However, communicating that love goes beyond expressing emotion. You are commanded to walk in love as a continuous lifestyle, for love is the integral mark of a disciple (John 13:34,35). You are capable of communicating love to your friends because Jesus has first communicated His love to you (John 15:12). He demonstrated the sacrificial extent of genuine love by surrendering His life (verse 13). You communicate an attitude of love to the death each time you sacrifice your own needs and wants for the greater need of a friend.

2–6.  Why did the Lord select real love for each other as the mark of true Christians? How well do you display this mark?

Jesus further illustrated the seriousness of communicating love when an expert in the law questioned Him about the greatest commandment. The Lord gave two of them—the first to love God fully, and the second to love others as much as self (Matthew 22:39). The love of a Christian friend is both a deep and abiding commitment and obedience to the greatest commandment.

**2–7.** *Why do you think your loving others is so important to the Lord that He called it the second greatest commandment?*

David and Jonathan also illustrate the value of faithfulness in friendship. Jonathan's father, King Saul, was jealous of David. His anger placed Jonathan in a precarious position, for Saul had determined to take David's life (1 Samuel 19:1). But Jonathan was faithful to his friend. Risking the wrath of his own father, Jonathan mediated a successful reconciliation between David and Saul (19:4–7). When that reconciliation was short-lived, Jonathan faithfully agreed to speak again on David's behalf (20:1–13). They then agreed to a second and more solemn covenant, pledging mutual protection for one another, even to their descendants (verses 12–16).

When a friend's life is under attack, because of personal behavior or by circumstances beyond his or her control, you may be tempted to forsake the friendship until calmer times prevail. While it may be easier to withdraw for a time, it is your duty as a friend to demonstrate faithfulness by supporting him or her through difficult times. As adversity strengthened the faithfulness of David and Jonathan, so your friendships can deepen, even prosper, during trials.

2–8.    *How have you experienced the deepening of a friendship in the middle of a crisis? How is your relationship with this friend stronger because of what you endured together?*

# Chapter Review

The crowning mark of Christian friendship is a willingness to be selfless instead of selfish. This quality highlights every scriptural example of great friendship. In contrast, you may be taking more from relationships than you give. While you need the love and support of godly friends, you also need to respond to them with love and support.

2–9.    *Can your friends depend on you or must they look to others, even unsaved acquaintances, for support? How do you feel about your answer?*

Follow the Lord's example of self-denial and sacrifice. Be a godly friend who will strive to love and support others, no matter what the cost. While it is true that not every person you meet will become a close companion, each of them has the potential of becoming an eternal friend in Christ.

**Friends are responsible to provide spiritual strength during crises.**

# Ministering To Each Other

Sorrow comes unexpectedly, success eludes, and tribulation falls on both the just and the unjust. Should the certainty of crises cause you to despair? In no way! Heartaches, failure, and hardship are merely opportunities for you to give and receive ministry from godly friends. Jesus never fails, and He is your source of strength. You can show His love when you reach out to others. Through Christ, you can successfully minister to the spiritual needs of friends in crisis.

## Comforting During Sorrow

One scriptural example of comforting friends started with what seemed to be callous disregard—John 11:1–7. But when the ordeal was over, Jesus proved to be a powerful example of comfort to some of His closest friends.

The siblings Mary, Martha, and Lazarus all enjoyed a close relationship with Jesus. So when Lazarus became deathly ill, it was natural for Mary and Martha to turn to Him. Imagine their grief when Jesus did not come immediately (verse 6), leaving Lazarus to die and be buried. The sisters must have been wounded by and angry at Jesus for His fatal delay. But from His vantage point, it was all part of God's plan for Lazarus and his sisters (verse 4).

During times of sorrow, many people do not clearly see what God is doing in their lives. A comforting friend helps you to look beyond the darkness to the coming dawn. You may not be able to offer specific answers for the tragedy your friend faces, but you can affirm God's trustworthy nature.

**3–1.** **What can you do that might encourage a friend who needs the Lord's intervention, but is faced with His delay?**

When Jesus arrived in Bethany, He could have started explaining why He had not come earlier. Instead, He allowed the sisters to vent their grief and frustration (verses 28–32). As you comfort your sorrowing friends, it is important that you allow them to express their emotions in their own way. Jewish culture encouraged loud and prolonged weeping, often within a large group (verse 33). One sorrowing friend may need to talk constantly. Another may withdraw in silence. No matter how they choose to mourn, they need to know the comfort of your presence will continue.

Jesus was a compassionate friend to Mary and Martha. He wept with the sisters (verses 35,36). But His compassion went beyond emotion to action. He had power to raise the dead. It was God's will to be glorified in this way and the miracle took place (verses 38–44).

You cannot claim to be as compassionate as the Savior is, nor are you as discerning and powerful as He is. Yet as His presence and power comforted the sisters in Bethany, so they can move through you today to comfort your friends.

*3–2.* *How have you experienced the Lord's helping you to comfort a friend? What did it feel like?*

When you do not know what to say or how to behave around those who mourn, God will guide you. You can also actively participate in their emotions as instructed in Romans 12:15. You cannot feel exactly what they feel, but you may have gone through other situations in which you needed the comfort of your Heavenly Father (2 Corinthians 1:3). The lessons you learned in those valleys can be translated into comfort for others who are sorrowing (verse 4). You do not need to have had an identical sorrow. Your experience does not provide comfort; the overflow of Christ's comfort through you does (verse 5).

*3–3.* *What personal experiences could you draw on to empathize with a friend in major sorrow?*

The sorrowful need you to be a friend who will remain firmly convinced that God is sovereign, that His grace is all they need, and He will produce godly character in them (verses 6,7). When a friend's faith wavers through sorrow, your faith can remain steadfast on his or her behalf.

**3–4.   What friend do you know who is dealing with a recent tragedy? What could you do to bring comfort?**

# Encouraging After Failure

Those closest to Jesus knew failure as well as sorrow. The disciples had happily served Jesus through more than 3 years of ministry, but found themselves after their Master's arrest and crucifixion without a leader and lacking hope. They did not even have their pride: they had abandoned their Lord at His most vulnerable moment. Even after the joy of knowing that Jesus had risen from death, they still struggled finding the right direction for their lives. A catchless night of fishing on the Lake of Galilee reflected this emptiness.

Read what happened the next morning in John 21 to see how Jesus encouraged those burdened by failure. He did not just tell them He loved them; He showed them. When He shouted out to the disciples to cast their nets one more time, the resulting abundance of fish in those once-empty nets caused hope to burn again in their hearts (verses 4–6).

3–5. *What do you think this miraculous catch said to the disciples about how Jesus felt about them?*

Peter had special need for encouragement. Out of fear for his own safety following Jesus' arrest, Peter had denied three times knowing the Master. Peter had repented, but he still undoubtedly felt unworthy to take his place again as a leader among Christ's followers.

Jesus knew of Peter's self-doubts and guilty conscience. So He pulled the disciple aside to reaffirm his standing as a leader of God's people (verses 15–17).

3–6. *Why do you think Jesus had Peter repeat his love for Jesus three times? What would this have meant to Peter?*

In ministering to friends who have failed, you must also encourage them to learn from the experience. Might God be attempting to sift the chaff of ungodly habits, motives, or attitudes from their lives? You can gently suggest these as possibilities, lest they fall into the same failure again.

3–7.   *What friend do you have who has failed God's standards
       and feels unworthy to serve Him anymore? How could
       Jesus' reaffirmation of Peter help you minister to this
       friend?*

You cannot erase the failures of your friends, but you can
help them get back to the place where God once worked
greatly in their lives. If they recognize their spiritual need and
repent, their restoration to fruitful work for God is possible.

# Support During Hardship

You will probably have opportunity many times over to
comfort grieving friends and restore friends who have failed
in some way. But by far the most common way you will serve
friends is supporting them through tough times.

The apostle Paul faced countless hardships. At times, he
felt abandoned by those he had considered friends. But more
often he found faithful friends by his side. You will read about
two such friends in this chapter.

According to 2 Timothy 1:16, one called Onesiphorus
"refreshed" Paul during his imprisonment. The Greek word
used in this verse implies the continued act of giving another
rest. Moreover, Onesiphorus had a history of being there
when Paul was in difficult situations (verse 18).

Supporting a friend enduring hardship requires persistent
love. Many times, the circumstances of the hardship are

beyond your friend's control; there is rarely a set time when the trial will be over. Your responsibility is to continue to minister to your friend as long as there is a need.

*3–8.* *Why do you think many people give up helping their friends through trying times? Why is this so unfortunate?*

A second example of supportive friends is the Philippian church (Philippians 4:11–13). As the Philippians ministered financially to Paul, he ministered spiritually in return. You may enjoy supporting friends during hardship, but are uncomfortable when they support you. Paul showed the importance of both aspects of ministry.

The Philippian believers also recognized that they had a responsibility to minister even if others did not follow their example (verses 15,16). Paul assured them their gifts had been received and accepted by God himself (verses 17,18). Those outside the situation may not understand your support of friends in hardship. Your duty, however, is to minister to those friends as to the Lord.

*3–9.* *Describe a time you were the only person supporting a friend who was going through trying circumstances.*

It must be noted that hardship may also take the form of spiritual battles. Often, those in the throes of temptation are ashamed to ask for help and may be overtaken by the sin. When you become aware of a struggle, you must quickly help that friend be restored to God (Galatians 6:1). Operating in Jesus' love means you will share a friend's spiritual burden, no matter how shameful or debilitating the sin (verse 2).

**3–10.** **Do you have a friend who is struggling against temptation and needs your encouragement, prayer, and advice? What can you do this week to help this friend overcome sin?**

# Chapter Review

Sorrow, failure, and hardship will probably come to you many times in your life. Each time, you would benefit from the support and encouragement of a godly friend. Do for your friends what you would want them to do for you. As a Christian friend, shoulder the yoke beside them so none is crushed beneath life's load. Helping each other as friends is a privilege. Practice it cheerfully and often.

# Part Two

# Communicating Effectively

This is the communication age. Phones, faxes, e-mail, and the Internet have made it easy to get a message to just about anyone. Increasing the quantity of communication, however, has not increased the quality of what is communicated.

The damage done by the misuse of communication is great, but the stakes get higher when communication is seen from a spiritual perspective. As a Christian, the things you say can affect the eternal destinies of those around you. If you are perceived as dishonest or slanderous, what you share with others about salvation will not be believed.

In this unit, you will look at aspects of communication and how you can best glorify the Lord and edify others in the things you say. Chapter 4 will urge you to be committed to telling the truth and avoid any kind of deception. In the next chapter, you will be reminded of the power of your words. The unit concludes with a chapter presenting the need to be frank and sensitive in speaking your mind.

**By trading deceit for honesty, you become more like Jesus.**

# Telling The Truth

As you read in the previous chapters, relationships are important. God made you to be with others. So it is vital that you do everything possible to keep those relationships healthy and open. Sincerity, honesty, and pure intentions combine to form the foundation for real communication that helps, not hinders, all relationships.

## Allowing No Half-Truths

4–1.  *How has less-than-fully-honest communication harmed one of your friendships? Why do you think what was said was so harmful?*

There is a common-sense reason for telling only the whole truth. Good communication is based on trust, which in turn requires truthfulness. Many people, even some Christians, are willing to shade the truth, saying what they think others want to hear instead of what is true. Reasons for such deceit vary: a person may be trying to spare your feelings or that person may be twisting the truth for his or her own personal gain or exaltation. Regardless of the motive involved, every deception reduces trust.

*4–2.    How would you rate your "honesty quotient" with coworkers on a 1 to 10 scale (10 being highly honest)? How are you with family members? What about close friends?*

As a believer, you must consider an even more important reason for honest communication: God requires you to be trustworthy. Whether you are completely honest affects more than your relationships with others; it makes a difference in the relationship you have with the Lord.

*4–3.    How might shading the truth hurt your relationship with God?*

In Psalm 52, David clearly stated that God will judge those who practice telling a tainted version of truth. Just like Doeg, the subject of this Psalm, deceitful people boast about their evil deeds (verse 1), misrepresent facts and events to their own benefit (verse 2), and prefer lies to the truth (verse 3). As David warned Doeg, God will judge harshly those who practice deception (verse 5).

4–4.　*In your opinion, was David too hard on Doeg for his deceit? What does your answer indicate about your tolerance or intolerance of lies?*

God values honesty. Proverbs 12:19 and 22 give assurance that God will bless the truthful forever. Those who have lying tongues will not have eternal life (see Revelation 21:8). But those who practice truthfulness will be the delight of the Lord. What a difference there is between those who practice deceit and lying and those who hold to and communicate only the truth.

4–5.　*Relate an experience you had in which God blessed you for being honest when lying would have been easy to do.*

In Ephesians 4:25, Paul related a very important teaching about truthfulness and relationships. One way you prove you have left your previous sinful life to live for God is by being truthful with others. Verses 22–24 explain that Christians must put off the old man—the former way of life—and put on the new man—the new life in Christ. One change that must occur is the replacement of falsehood with truthfulness (verse 25). This is not the only change God requires, but it is an indicator of your new life in Christ.

4–6.   **How has your desire to be honest increased since you accepted Christ? Has this desire for truth grown along with your spiritual maturity?**

# Avoiding Deception's Trap

If you doubted it before, you now know you must avoid telling lies and half-truths, no matter how innocent they may seem. But you also need to keep yourself from becoming the victim of deceit. Sadly, one of the main areas in which you must be on guard is your church.

In Romans 16:17,18, Paul warned about teachers who would infiltrate the church to cause division by deception. The deceit came in two forms—unscriptural teaching and "smooth talk and flattery." Both kinds of lies eroded the church's unity and purity.

4–7.   *How have you seen outsiders spread false or controversial doctrines in a church and ruin its unity? What was done to end the lies and restore unity and biblical truth?*

Differences of opinion—about doctrine and other, less important, matters—exist in every church. As long as the fundamental doctrines of Scripture are widely accepted, such differences are not a problem. The trouble comes when some overemphasize the differences or attempt to argue everyone into agreeing with only one view—theirs. Once winning the argument becomes more important than maintaining unity or honesty, a congregation can fall prey to deception's trap. Truth is easily cast aside for overstatement, exaggeration, manipulation, and character assassination.

4–8.   *As implied in Romans 16:18, how can spiritual discernment help you recognize and resist deceit in your church?*

According to Ephesians 5:6–12, lying is something unsaved people do that believers must do no longer. Paul even warned Christians to break ties with those who continue to deceive others despite their supposed repentance and new life in Christ (verses 6,7). The exchange of lies for truth must parallel the exchange of spiritual darkness for divine light (verse 8). These exchanges are what sets the behavior of God's people apart from those who do not know Him.

**4–9.** *What friends of yours make a practice of lying? How can you remove yourself from their influence without making them feel you are rejecting them personally?*

Sometimes the one you end up deceiving with half-truths is yourself. Many people convince themselves they do not need God. But both Romans 3:23—"All have sinned and fall short of the glory of God"—and 1 John 1:8—"If you say that you have no sin, you deceive yourself"—confirm that every person needs God's mercy.

Even as a Christian, you may have deceived yourself into thinking that you can live for God in your own power, that you only need God's presence during trials, or that you have reached the point when sin no longer tempts you. These lies may make you feel better about yourself, but they can only harm you in the end. You must admit to yourself and to God that you need help living in obedience to God's Word and Spirit. Paul freely admitted he struggled with sin but was quick to point out that Christ provided the victory (see Romans 6, 7, and 8). John wrote: "If we confess our sins, he is faithful and just and will forgive us our sins and purify us from all unrighteousness" (1 John 1:9).

*4–10. What sins have you lied to yourself about, saying they really are not bad enough to warrant repentance? Take the time after recording them to confess them to God.*

# Committing Yourself To Truth

Knowing lying is wrong and recognizing how destructive it can be is not enough: you must commit to speaking the truth in your daily activities. This commitment is essential to your communication as a Christian.

*4–11. Write out a commitment before God to be truthful in all your communication.*

What happens when you are truthful? As the apostle Paul explained in Ephesians 4:14,15, truthfulness is an important component of the maturing process of believers. The more you speak the truth, the easier it will be to recognize and avoid lies, helping you to grow in Christ along with other believers.

# Chapter Review

Honest communication is the cornerstone of every solid relationship. As you have learned in this chapter, practicing deceit invites God's judgment, while speaking the truth strengthens friendships and brings God's blessings. Live out the commitment you have made, taking every opportunity you find to tell the truth in love.

**You can kill or heal another's spirit with your tongue.**

# Weighing Your Words

Have you ever been struck in the head with a rock? It is painful, but the possibility of sustaining lasting damage is even more frightening.

Have you ever been hit in the heart by gossip or slander? The pain is just as real, and the emotional injury caused by gossip can last a lifetime.

*5–1. Describe how you feel when others gossip about you.*

Words can hurt. They can damage another's spirit, mind, and emotions. Words can be a dangerous weapon, but they can also be a means to inner healing. The decision to use words that hurt or heal is yours.

# Putting A Lid On Gossip

Some people intentionally broadcast information about others that should not be discussed, but such people are in the minority. Most people fall into gossip without realizing they have gone beyond discussing a situation to analyzing another's private life and personality.

5–2.   *Why do you think it is so easy for many people to gossip about others?*

This kind of accidental backstabbing happens in the Church as well. In his letter to a young pastor named Timothy, Paul warned about young widows having too much time on their hands and becoming gossips (1 Timothy 5:11–13). The same pitfall awaits anyone, not just a widow, who had more spare time than could be filled productively.

5–3.   *When do you share gossip or listen to it the most—during casual conversations with close friends or when you are busy? What can you learn from this about one way to help prevent gossiping?*

No matter why gossip happens, it always hurts! Gossip destroys relationships. Since relationships are the strength of any church, gossip by both men and women can destroy a congregation. You can remember personally how it hurts to be the one others have gossiped about—like being cut up into small pieces for general distribution.

5–4.   *Discuss a time you learned others had been talking about you behind your back. What did you feel like? How did their gossip affect your relationships with them?*

Solomon wrote insightfully about the way gossip affects relationships: it betrays confidences (Proverbs 11:13). The information gossiped in public is often gained in private. Mutual honesty is the foundation for any relationship. Gossip's betrayal of trust erodes this foundation. You need to feel secure in communicating with others or you will not be open enough with others to communicate fully and truly.

5–5.   *Have you wounded a friend by telling others things he or she told you in confidence? What happened to the friendship? What did you do (or can you do) to repair it?*

Gossip continues its destruction by causing hard feelings: it "digs up evil" (Proverbs 16:27). Almost before you realize it is happening, a church can divide into separate camps, with all relationships strained and even close friends divided. Hard feelings then infect other relationships associated with the relationships first affected. Can you see how gossip could eventually destroy an entire church?

5–6.  *Is your church being attacked by the gossip being spread among its members? What can you do to bring healing between those who gossiped and those who were hurt by it?*

# Preventing Slander

Just as unchecked gossip damages relationships, slander damages once good reputations. According to Proverbs 11:9, one who slanders others has effectively severed his or her relationship with God. The word translated "hypocrite" refers to one without any internal good and separated from God.

Scripture takes a very definite stand against slander. In Matthew 5:21,22, Jesus gave one of the clearest indications of how severe a sin slander is. Equating slander with murder, the highest form of disregard against human life, Jesus warned that those who destroy others with their tongue are "subject to judgment" and "in danger of the fire of hell." The truth behind Jesus' three parallel statements is clear: you can kill someone's spirit just as quickly with your tongue as you can kill physically with a knife. God condemns slander, the sin of the tongue, along with murder.

5–7. *Why do you think the Bible speaks so harshly against slanderers? How does this make you feel as one who has been wounded by slander? What do you feel if you have slandered others?*

Gossip hurts, slander kills, and sadly, both happen within the Church. Why? Because your congregation and every other one in the world is a group made up of vastly differing types of people existing on many different levels of Christian maturity. As some learn to control their hurtful words, others come who have not yet learned this control.

5–8. *What can you do to help a Christian friend who slanders and gossips to change?*

What can you do to defend yourself against slander? Read 1 Peter 3:16. While the context is that of sinners maligning Christians, the verse is equally applicable when one is slandered by fellow believers. Regardless of its source, slander can only be fought with the truth. If you are the object of slander and gossip when all you have done is what God requires, try not to worry about it. A pure life is the only defense necessary (verse 16).

**5–9.** *What would you tell the believer whose godly reputation is being unfairly attacked?*

# Healing With Loving Words

When you remove gossip and slander from your daily communication, you need to replace them with loving words. Paul called for this kind of transformation in Ephesians 4:31,32. It is not easy. It requires you to demonstrate the kindness and forgiveness God has shown to you.

**5–10.** *Why should the forgiveness Christ gave you affect the way you speak to others?*

You are called to act toward others in the way that you wish to be treated. Probably about the time you obey this call someone will abuse you. It is almost a given. If you want to please God, you must continue to do good anyway.

Forgiveness is another requirement. Jesus said you must forgive (Matthew 6:14,15). Forgiveness is not easy, but Paul said, since God acted toward you in forgiveness, He expects you to act the same way—forgiving others freely (Ephesians 4:32). This is necessary to establish right relationships.

**5–11. How have you seen forgiveness heal a friendship damaged by slander?**

As you choose to establish right relationships you also choose to use gracious speech. Colossians 4:6 says that your conversation must be filled with favor and have a preserving quality. You should converse in such a manner as to build others up. Gossip and slander certainly cannot edify anyone. You will keep (preserve) right relationships with encouraging and healing words just as salt is used to preserve food.

Peter gave the key to using healing, encouraging words in 1 Peter 4:8—love. This love is special. It is not a love that is dependent on or affected by outside influences. Situations cannot change this love; instead, it changes situations. Such genuine love is from God. With the help of the Holy Spirit, the believer can demonstrate this love to others. Godly love works to heal the hurts of gossip and slander. Jesus already proved that on Calvary. He still proves it as He stands ever at the Father's side defending Christians from the accusations (gossip and slander) of Satan.

*5–12. In what relationship do you need the miraculous love of God to be stirred in you? What will you do to express that love to one who has wounded you with gossip or slander?*

# Chapter Review

Gossip hurts, slander kills, but love heals. You are living in a time when the Church needs encouragement and healing. As a believer, you must determine to use words that bring these results. What you say really does matter.

God's love is the means of developing healing speech. The Holy Spirit will guide you in the use of God's love. Pray for His special anointing to equip you to combat the ravages of careless and evil speech.

There are times when giving constructive criticism is necessary.

# Speaking Your Mind

You have examined dishonesty, gossip, and slander. Having considered several ways you should not communicate, it is time for you to look at some biblical guidelines for positive communication.

As a Christian, your communication with others must be characterized by openness, transparency, and a willingness to confront issues. Yet these three characteristics of healthy communication can be misused. Being open and transparent can lead you into unhealthy self-disclosure. You can confront differences you have with others in the wrong spirit. The key to successful communication is allowing God to guide you in how you apply each point.

## Being Open With Others

For many people, a large obstacle to being open is the risk of being misunderstood. There is always the fear that others might not receive correctly what you are trying to share with them. Being misunderstood is not only embarrassing; it can cause problems.

51

*6–1.   Why do you think it is so easy for people to mistake open communication for arrogance or rudeness?*

Joseph's brothers hated him because their father Jacob showed him favoritism. This in itself caused great problems. But when Joseph related two dreams that seemed to indicate he would rule over his family (Genesis 37:5–11), his brothers jumped to the conclusion that Joseph coveted power over them. His willingness to be open with his family caused them to hate him even more than they had previously.

The Bible does not tell why Joseph told the dreams to his family. He does not seem to have been gloating over them. Rather, he seems to have been either just sharing the dreams or seeking understanding as to what the dreams meant. Joseph did not understand what was in store for him at this point either. Joseph went to his family because he needed to find some answers; what he found was anger and resentment.

*6–2.   Relate a time you were mistaken when you were simply being open. What did you do to correct the misconception?*

When you reveal to others your honest needs or questions, it is possible they will abuse instead of assist. Is it better, then, to keep your needs and questions to yourself? It may seem emotionally safe, but it is not wise to be closed to those around you. If you stay safe and rely on yourself exclusively to handle problems, you might never find solutions or get the assistance you need. You need the strength found through the support of those who care for you. To get effective prayer assistance, you need to be open in asking for prayer. If you have troubling questions, you need to seek those who might help you find answers. You must determine to be open and trust that God will accomplish His purpose.

6–3.   *What need or question do you have about which you know you must be open with one or more close friends? Why is the desire for help and support greater than the tendency to keep the need or question to yourself?*

By Genesis 50:15–21, the dreams had been fulfilled. Joseph's brothers had bowed to him. But Jacob had died and Joseph's brothers were afraid for what he would do. Joseph was now in a position to avenge the wrongs he had suffered at the hands of his brothers many years before. Two words expose Joseph's transparent nature when he realized his brothers' fear: "Joseph wept" (verse 17). Joseph had revealed himself so openly to his family that it hurt him to believe they still felt he would harm them.

Joseph cared for all of those in his charge. He assured his family that God used the events they had meant for evil to not only preserve that family, but all of the people in that area of the world. This attitude of openness was one of the reasons God could use Joseph in the way He did.

**6–4.**   *How have you seen a person's openness lead to great things that would have been impossible otherwise?*

# Confronting Carefully

There are times when you are called to be open in an even more direct manner than sharing personal information. Believers have to deal with differences among themselves. The ability to confront issues directly, and do so in a godly manner, is very necessary for continued unity.

**6–5.**   *What friend of yours needs to be confronted about things he or she is doing? Have you found it difficult to bring up the subject?*

If you are like most people, your first reaction to discord or misbehavior in others is to avoid confrontation. Many people would rather ignore problems, even great ones, than deal with them. But this reaction only compounds the problem. Sometimes you need to confront whatever is causing the problem to get rid of the problem.

6–6. **How can you tactfully and lovingly confront your friend about what he or she is doing wrong?**

Paul had to deal with an issue involving Peter (Galatians 2:11–16). When Peter came to Antioch, he fellowshiped with the Gentile believers, eating their food and worshiping with them. But when Jewish Christians arrived from Jerusalem, Peter disassociated himself from the Gentiles. What was the proper thing for Paul to do? Peter was such an important figure in the Church. Could Paul actually confront him? Paul knew that the truth had to be established, and he confronted Peter and settled the problem.

6–7. **What can you learn about proper confrontation from Paul's confronting Peter?**

Solomon provided sound wisdom about handling conflict through confrontation. A very real risk of confrontation is creating an angry response. The key to dealing with anger is found in a gentle, conciliatory approach to the issue (Proverbs 15:1). If you learn to communicate in this gentle spirit, you can settle most problems quickly. Retaliating in harshness only stirs up more anger. Gentleness has the potential of turning aside even the hottest rage.

6–8.   *When have you seen confrontation poorly handled and the situation made worse? How was the outcome different in a situation in which the confrontation was done gently and tactfully?*

# Being Transparent

The idea of transparency, like many other communication issues, can be misused. Some feel that true honesty involves sharing every intimate detail of one's life. "Being transparent" has become a catch phrase in some circles used to intimidate people into baring their souls.

Your communication characteristics need to be developed using Christ as your model. Jesus did not share all of His thoughts with anyone. He kept the Pharisees off balance with enigmatic answers to their dishonest questions. His parables were intended to filter spiritual information to those prepared to receive it. Even with His disciples, Jesus did not reveal everything. What did transparency mean for Christ? It meant He let others see through Him and look to the Father.

6–9. *Why is it more important that people see the Lord than the inner workings of your heart?*

From John 14:1–11, it is obvious the disciples did not understand Jesus' kind of transparency. Although He had told them His purpose for being on earth was to declare the Father to them, both Thomas and Philip's questions show that the disciples still had much to learn. Jesus wanted them to realize that they, as His followers, could also help others see God. This is Christ's goal for all believers.

6–10. *How can God the Father be seen in your life when you are transparent about your experiences, hopes, and fears?*

Obviously, you can only reveal Christ by your transparency when He truly fills every aspect of your life. One way to be real with others and still show them Christ is found in Colossians 3:16. You must have the word of Christ—His commands—living in you. If you are full of Christ's words, you can provide needed direction and edification for others whenever you share from your own experiences.

6–11.  *What have you learned about the Lord through your trials and mistakes that would benefit friends with whom you were transparent?*

# Chapter Review

When you follow God, you can receive divine guidance in your communication with others. You can be open and still trust God to bring about His will in spite of hostile reactions. You can confront differences with others, again relying on God to give you wisdom. With God's Word filling your life, His life will be seen in all that you say and do. You will become transparent, and people will truly see Christ in you.

# Part Three

# Serving Others

Perhaps you had the following experience, or one similar to it: You have been searching for a way to serve God more fully. You have devoted extra time to Bible study, prayer, and church attendance. You keep expecting to receive some kind of revelation that will point your life in the right direction. Instead of some glory-filled chance to serve with distinction, the first opportunity for service is an invitation to teach a Sunday School class, volunteer to do custodial work at your church, participate in a hospital visitation program, or be a part of some other less-than-glamorous work.

Throughout your life, you will find many opportunities for service. Many of these chances to serve will be small and associated with mundane events. But being faithful in these acts of service will help you grow spiritually. This unit will present you with basic guidelines for Christian service. When you apply these guidelines, you will find that God can use you for His glory in limitless ways.

# Learning From Christ

If you stood on a street corner and asked passersby if they viewed themselves as servants, a fairly typical response might be: "A servant? Who, me? Actually, you see, I'm a…." If you were to walk the top floor of a major corporation, you would pass by office doors bearing a variety of titles—chairman, CEO, president, vice president, director—but none that read: "Servant."

Secular society is not warm to the idea of servanthood. Servant's quarters are relegated to the basements of the social structure. There reside the commoners, whose roles are to cater and pander to the needs, whims, and fancies of the upper levels. In the biblical record, however, you can find a much different order, one where "Servant's Quarters" would designate a place of honor. The chief example is One whose pedigree reads King of kings and Lord of lords.

## Serving With Compassion

Understanding servanthood requires that you examine Jesus' earthly life and ministry and ask, "What motivated His servant heart?" Finding the answer is important, because the same thing must motivate you if you are to be like Him.

**7-1.    Before looking at any Bible passages, what do you think motivated Jesus to serve others?**

**7-2.    Do you believe motivation is important when discussing the need to serve others? Why or why not?**

Mark 6:30–44 records an event that followed a very busy day for Jesus and His disciples. Exhausted, they sought to get away for a while and relax. They went by boat to a solitary place; at least this was their plan (verse 32). On their arrival at this place, they discovered the crowds had scurried on foot around the end of the lake and were waiting for them (verse 33). They wanted to hear more from Jesus.

It is doubtful you would have responded to this situation with joy and loving concern. Yet when Jesus saw the crowds, He displayed an emotion central to servanthood: He had

compassion on them. He saw them as wandering sheep with
no one to lead them (verse 34).

7–3. *What is the difference between pity and compassion?*
*Would pity have necessarily motivated Jesus to serve the*
*people? Why or why not?*



Compassion erases contempt. It looks past inconvenience
and zeroes in on opportunity. It looks for ways to help, to
make a difference in someone's life. Compassion can move
you beyond feeling sorry for someone to doing something
about it.

Jesus' concern for the people was not only spiritual, though
that was the peoples' most important need, and the one He
met first. He also cared that the peoples' stomachs were
empty. They were hungry, so He fed them (verses 35–42).

7–4. *List some other Bible passages that urge believers to*
*serve physical and emotional needs as well as spiritual*
*ones. How are you challenged by these verses?*

Feeding the 5,000 was as much a miracle of servanthood as it was one of supernatural provision. The Son of God whose power created the very earth these people stood on, was preparing a meal to quell their hunger pangs.

Compassion is a powerful motivation for service. It resides even in unregenerate humanity. Repeatedly, newspapers and news broadcasts have carried stories of people coming together when floods, fires, tornadoes, and hurricanes have wreaked havoc. Thousands of people, most of whom did not know one another, were moved by compassion and rallied to one another's aid.

**7–5.**   **What do you think Christians can learn from unbelievers about serving others out of compassion?**

Like the compassionate heart of Christ, a godly servant's heart breaks with concern for those caught in sin's ravages. It also sees all the needs of others—spiritual, social, emotional, physical. Compassion is essential to servanthood.

## Serving With Humility

Compassion is necessary to motivate you to serve others, but you must also develop humility. Being humble is an aspect of servanthood that makes it less palatable for many. Why is this? Because humility renders aid without thought of reward or notice.

7–6. *Do you typically do things for others because they need you to or because you want to be praised or rewarded for it? How can you improve your humility in serving others?*

John's gospel records an event that highlights this attitude in Christ, the chief example of servanthood. Chapter 13 finds Jesus Christ with His disciples on the eve of His crucifixion. They had gathered for a final Passover meal. Before the end of the meal, Jesus rose, removed His outer garments, wrapped himself in a towel, poured water in a basin, and proceeded to wash the disciples' feet, drying them with His towel (verses 4,5). Only a house servant performed this task.

When you consider what He knew about himself, Jesus' humble act is even more astounding. The Son of God, who knew that God the Father had put all things under His power, that He had come from God, and that He would soon return to the glories of heaven, washed dusty feet.

7–7. *How does knowing how far Jesus humbled himself to be a servant change your attitude about doing things for others that you feel are beneath you?*

# Serving Sincerely

As you have seen, you cannot pretend to be a servant. When service is not motivated by compassion tempered by humility, it smacks of "what's in it for me?"

**7–8.** *Have you ever been served by someone whose motives were selfish and insincere? How did recognizing his or her false motives affect the value of that service to you?*

In Matthew 20:20,21, the mother of James and John asked that her sons be given the privilege of being at Jesus' side in His kingdom. Verses 22–24 show that her sons were in full agreement with the proposition. James, John, and their mother exhibited the trappings of servanthood when they approached Jesus with their request. They knelt down before Him. Yet they had not internalized Jesus' earlier teaching about servanthood, where He had said those who humble themselves as little children will be the greatest in heaven's kingdom (18:4). They were still thinking in earthly terms—kings, kingdoms, and positions of importance. Since they were associated with the Lord, James and John felt they should have a right to prominence. Serving from a sincere heart was not in their thinking.

Jesus' reply was not meant to be scolding, but it was still straightforward: "You don't know what you are asking" (Matthew 20:22). Were they willing to experience all He would have to go through? They were quick to say yes, but Jesus knew better. Patiently, again, He dealt with the issue of servanthood from His perspective. If they wanted to be great, they had to learn to be servants first. You could paraphrase verses 26 and 27 this way: "The way up is down." God honors those willing to serve everyone else even if no one serves them.

7–9.  *What do you think of the concept that the way up is down? How is this possible?*

7–10. *Do you desire to be recognized or rewarded for serving others? Would you rather have others serve you? Do you find it easy to feel you are too important to do certain kinds of service or serve certain people? Why do you think these are such common struggles for Christians?*

A true servant acknowledges he or she is not above any job, regardless of its perceived importance. Servanthood is not about gaining status or recognition, but about giving yourself willingly for the good of others. Ultimately, Jesus exemplified sincere servanthood by giving His life for your redemption. He is now your exalted Lord and Savior, seated at the Father's right hand.

# Chapter Review

Biblical servanthood is a great mystery to the world. Their supreme objective is to make it to the top at any cost. Wealth, power, and prestige are pursued by every means possible, often without regard for the welfare of others. Yet many who have made it to the top in terms of earthly gain have found it to be a lonely, desolate place.

Conversely, those willing to put on the towel of servanthood can find great joy, fulfillment, and satisfaction. Hebrews 12:2 states that Jesus, "for the joy set before him endured the cross, scorning its shame, and sat down at the right hand of the throne of God."

There is joy in serving. Seek to follow Christ's pattern of servanthood in your life. When you live life in the order of Jesus, Others, and You, it always spells JOY.

7–11.  *What can you do this week to realign your priorities and find greater joy in serving others as Christ did?*

# Finding Places To Serve

"Help Wanted." At least once, you have probably searched this section of the newspaper or have looked for such signs in business windows. You needed to find a place to serve, to earn a living. And you most likely discovered there were jobs to be found for those willing to work. Spiritual help-wanted signs are posted everywhere—in the home, in the church, and in the community. There is no lack of places in which you can serve Christ and others at the same time.

## Serving In The Home

The home is the primary context for spiritual training and ministry. In the home, basic principles of Christian living and serving are taught and modeled.

Scripturally, serving in the home must be grounded in a relationship with Jesus, who personally conveyed this truth while visiting the sisters Mary and Martha (Luke 10:38–42). Martha was consumed with trying to serve Jesus, so much so that she was more concerned with the details of her service than the with the One she was serving. Mary, on the other hand, seemed to understand that knowing and learning from Jesus was far more important than doing things for Him.

**8–1.** *Are you so busy doing things for Jesus that you fail to spend time with Him in your home individually and with your family? If so, what can you do to change this?*

With proper priorities in place, in what ways can you serve in your home? One practical way might be caring for family members unable to adequately care for themselves. When Paul wrote 1 Timothy 5, the only places senior adults could turn to for help were their families and the local church. Paul was adamant that the first responsibility for caring for the elderly falls squarely on their family members. Taking care of a parent is, in essence, paying back all the years he or she invested in your life and cared for you. Although it makes great demands of you, the Lord can help you to accept those difficulties and determine to see caring for a parent as one way you can serve in your home.

**8–2.** *Have you helped take care of an aging parent? How did you keep a servant's attitude?*

Another way to minister at home is to open it to others. This can be as involved as hosting a foreign exchange student or as simple as having the neighbors over for dinner.

8–3.   What are some other ways you could serve others this week by showing hospitality in your home? What about this month?

First Peter 4:9 instructs you to offer hospitality "without grumbling." Hospitality is often practiced today out of social obligation, not the desire for fellowship. Many people would rather watch television and eat carryout than have guests over for dinner. But people need social interaction. Your home can be an effective avenue to help meet this need.

8–4.   How else can a believer serve in his or her home? What difference might it make to view marriage and parenting as acts of service?

# Serving In The Church

If you are looking for help-wanted signs, you can find plenty of them in your church. Whether your church is a megachurch, a suburban fellowship, a rural congregation, or a newly planted outreach, there are always jobs and ministries that need to be filled.

*8–5.   List the ways are you currently serving in your local church.*

Sadly, the church often has the greatest unmet needs. Instead of answering Jesus' command, "Feed My sheep," some Christians demand, "Feed this sheep!" Being fed spiritually is an important reason to gather with other believers, but there must be some people who help to feed others. Scripturally, every person needs to participate in this. The beauty of such a system is that, when you serve others, you are often fed more richly than you could have imagined.

*8–6.   How have you experienced the paradox of gaining more from serving in the church than the effort you put into it?*

Paul posted a sample help-wanted list in Romans 12:3–8. Seven kinds of ministry are outlined—prophesying, serving, teaching, encouraging, contributing to needs, leadership, and showing mercy. No one person can do everything that needs to be done in a congregation. This is why Paul emphasized, "If a man's gift is…" (verse 6). God desires to use you in ways that align with the strengths, talents, and interests He has given you.

8–7.   *What gifts do you have? What are your talents and interests?*

Many believers, caught up in the corporate mentality, tend to assign levels of importance to various avenues of service. They desire labels, titles, and name tags that indicate they are people of importance. But God judges the value of service in the church on the bases of willingness and obedience, not human levels of importance.

8–8.   *If your service in church has reflected a corporate mentality instead of biblical servanthood, what practical things can you do this week to help you change your motivation?*

# Serving The Public

Home and church are natural opportunities for service, but God also needs servants in the public sector—local, state, and national politics, as well as school boards, parent-teacher associations and other local organizations that make an impact on a community's moral climate.

**8–9.** *How have you seen Christians in public leadership make a positive difference?*

**8–10.** *How could you become more involved in public service in your community, either as a leader or as a behind-the-scenes volunteer?*

Scripture refers to a number of godly people who were involved in important areas of public service. Among the most notable are Daniel and his three Hebrew friends. All of them had been carried into Babylonian captivity when King Nebuchadnezzar besieged and conquered Jerusalem. The king had intended to mold these exiles into Babylonians, but he failed when it came to the Hebrew captives. Committed to the one true God, they refused to be pressed into the mold, yet proved superior to the best of their pagan counterparts.

8–11. **What do Daniel 1:8; 2:17–19; 3:16–18; and 6:1–5 reveal about what motivated and guided these men in public service? How were they able to serve God in a pagan environment?**

Daniel and his friends were likely tempted to compromise their faith to ensure greater success, but they remained true to the Lord. Conformity and compromise are great temptations for Christians in the public arena, capable of driving a wedge between them and scriptural values. Believers working in public service need your prayers and encouragement.

Scripture also refers to others in public leadership. Erastus, whom Paul greeted in Romans 16:23, served as a director of public works. In Philippians 4:22, Paul sent greetings to those of Caesar's household, who held posts of government service. Each was a point of light in a dark world.

Sometimes Christians in the public arena, particularly in politics, are misunderstood and criticized. Sadly, resistance may come from fellow Christians more than from the public. Christians in public service need your prayers far more than your criticisms. They are important influences for the Lord. And you can be too if you pray for such opportunities.

*8–12.  List four Christians in any area of public service whom you
        will commit to pray for this week.*

# Chapter Review

When you review the opportunities to serve God through
your home, at church, and in the community, the question
quickly changes from "Where can I serve?" to "Where can I
not serve?" The help-wanted signs are posted all around you.
The only factors needed are willingness, obedience, and a
sensitivity to the voice of the Spirit.

God has gifted you with special abilities and talents.
Regardless of how spectacular or mundane you think they
may be, God can use your strengths in meaningful ways.

*8–13.  Take time to evaluate each of the arenas discussed in this
        study. Reaffirm below how you can more effectively serve
        others in your home, church, and community.*

**Follow Christ's example by caring for people who are hurting.**

# Helping The Hurting

Christian service extends beyond the relatively safe and simple world of home and church. If you desire to serve as Jesus did, you will have to find a way to help those wrestling against pain, disease, violence, hunger, and moral failure.

As a believer in Jesus Christ, you have the unique privilege and responsibility of serving people who are hurting. The Church exists to help people in need, just as Christ did while on earth. You are Christ's hands extended to meet their needs.

9–1.  *Does the Bible really call believers to do more than share the gospel with the lost? What about our responsibility to help those hurting people who are fellow believers?*

# Praying For The Sick

The cause of a person's emotional turmoil is sometimes a physical ailment. Some people, even believers, try to blame God for their illness because they feel singled out by Him for suffering.

But according to the Bible, sickness has been a part of the human experience since the Fall and is not caused by God. On the contrary, He has repeatedly proven in Scripture His ability and desire to heal those hurt by illness or disease.

**9–2.** *What is your favorite account of healing in the Bible? Why is this your favorite?*

**9–3.** *How could you use your favorite biblical account of healing to encourage a friend who is struggling with sickness?*

Reminding the sick of God's healing power may lift the spirits of those demoralized by illness, but you can do much more for them than that. According to Jesus himself, you can pray for the sick and see them healed.

After His miraculous resurrection and a 3-year ministry filled with healings, Jesus gave His followers His final orders for them to follow after He was gone (Mark 16:17,18). In that commission, Jesus outlined five signs that would follow those who believe in Him. Healing is one of these signs.

**9–4.** *Describe a healing you experienced or know about that God used to confirm His power to save.*

The apostle James penned special instructions for those who need healing (James 5:14–16.) The sick are to call on mature believers who have strong faith in Christ's promises to pray in faith. Does this mean you cannot pray for people to be healed or anoint them with oil if you are not an elder or a minister? Absolutely not! You have the privilege to pray for others' healing with confidence.

**9–5.** *Why do you think James included being forgiven for sins in a prayer for healing?*

# Caring For The Needy

Hurt and distress are not only caused by physical ailments. Many people are without the most basic necessities—food, clothing, and shelter. Economic crises caused by disability, unemployment, inadequate skills, or natural calamities can wreak havoc with a person's emotions, self-esteem, and faith in God's care for him or her.

Reaching people in these difficult circumstances is high on God's agenda. The forgotten, the disfranchised, and the downtrodden were ones Jesus Christ often touched during His earthly ministry. You are to do the same.

9–6.    *List five people you know who have been affected by economic or social hardships. What have you done lately to serve the needs of each of them?*

    •

    •

    •

    •

    •

In Matthew 25:31–40, Jesus said that in the end times there will be a separation of the sheep from the goats. Sheep will be welcomed into the kingdom of God; the goats will not. What will be the criteria for entrance? It will be practical acts of kindness to the needy—feeding the hungry, providing lodging for the stranger, clothing the naked, caring for the sick, and visiting the imprisoned.

Was Jesus saying you can get to heaven on the merit of your own good works for the needy? Not at all. He was just illustrating the importance of living out your professed love for God and others by actually doing something for them.

9–7.   What other Scripture passages can you think of that reveal how strongly Jesus felt about believers' responsibility to care for the needy? List them below.

This level of serving and caring is not easy. Most people shrink from getting involved in the problems of others. "I have enough of my own, thank you," they reply. Yet Jesus' parable of the final judgment demands a willingness to get your hands dirty, perhaps literally, and touch human need.

9–8.   What ministries of your local church could help you reach out to the needy, either saved or unsaved?

Interestingly, the six acts of service outlined in Matthew 25 are not typically "spiritual." Feeding, clothing, caring for the sick, visiting prisons, have little to do with doctrine. Yet when you perform these acts without thought of personal reward or merit, you fulfill the law of love. Only a relationship with Christ can inspire such a love for others. Only with this kind of love can you reach people who are forgotten—the poor, the mistreated, and the imprisoned.

**9-9.**   *Do you think Matthew 25 teaches you to minister only to the tangible needs and not spiritual ones? Why or why not?*

According to Hebrews 13:1–3, your service to the needy ought to be rendered as if you were the one needing the care. This passage is a reflection of the Golden Rule: treat others in the same way you want to be treated. Those who enjoy health and plenty could easily be in the place of the hurting and destitute. May your thankfulness for your own position in life motivate you to serve the less fortunate in love.

## Restoring Those Who Fail

Ministry to hurting people is undeniably the heartbeat of God. Scripture makes it clear that you must reach out to the sick and the needy. But your concern must not stop there. You are also to reach out to those believers who have failed by yielding to the temptation to sin.

The hurting who fail—morally, spiritually, emotionally, or otherwise—are often left to themselves to suffer alone. In a society where people want to be identified with the movers and shakers, one who has failed is often branded as a loser and is avoided.

*9–10. Have you found it easy to distance yourself from a Christian friend whose sins were exposed? Did this friend's repentance affect the way you felt about and acted toward him or her?*

John 18 presents a story of one disciple's failure. Pressed by accusers in the courtyard regarding his association with Jesus, Peter vehemently denied knowing Him. When Peter realized what he had done, he was filled with remorse and shame. He had failed.

*9–11. Are remorse and shame enough to receive forgiveness and restoration? If so, why? If not, what else is needed?*

Thankfully, Peter also repented. It was this repentance that allowed the conversation of John 21:15–17 to take place. In a post-Resurrection appearance, Jesus asked Peter a question central to restitution—"Do you love Me?" When Peter replied that he did, Jesus said, "Feed My sheep." In short, Jesus was telling Peter, "I know you've repented of your action. Reaffirm your devotion to Me and get on with doing what I have asked you to do."

9–12. How could you use John 21 to encourage a friend who has been restored but does not think God wants to work through him or her anymore?

# Chapter Review

Some sociologists use the term "cocooning"—shutting oneself off from others—to describe the social behavior of many people today. Regrettably, many believers do the same thing, keeping themselves from helping the hurting. But the Bible is clear: you must reach out and serve.

9–13. What will you do this week to leave your "cocoon" and serve the sick, the needy, and those who have failed?

# Part Four

# Sharing The Gospel

If a person discovered the remedy for AIDS but refused to tell anyone else, what would your opinion of him or her be? Regardless of how good his or her reasons were, you would likely consider him or her selfish and uncaring, hardly the kind of friend and servant this book has been talking about.

The world has been infected by the most fatal disease of all—sin. Sin infects every human being that has lived or will ever live. But there is a cure for this terrible disease. You, along with all other believers, have been commissioned by Jesus Christ to share His life-giving gospel.

This unit was not written to make you feel guilty, although you may experience the Spirit's conviction if you have not been making an effort to witness to others. To bolster your confidence, chapter 10 will remind you of the basics of the gospel. The next two chapters will encourage you with scriptural examples to witness unashamedly to both people you know and those you do not.

**The Bible is the best resource for knowing how to lead others to Christ.**

# Leading Someone
# To Christ

You have probably felt it before—the sweaty palms, the thumping heart, the feel of your blood pumping through the veins in your temples. The person in front of you is staring expectantly. You hear your voice cracking slightly as you try to express what sounded so eloquent in your mind: "Do you, that is, I mean, are you…would you read this tract later?" You can see the person shrugging why-not, but your brain is already plotting your escape. You are already starting to turn away as you thrust out a wrinkled tract and feel it pulled from your fingers. You catch the briefest eye contact and mumble, "God bless you" before melting as quickly as possible into the crowd around you.

Your experiences with witnessing have probably not been this bad. Yet for many Christians, the thought of confronting someone with his or her need for Jesus is intimidating, if not terrifying. Even for people who are used to witnessing, it can have its nervous moments.

This chapter may seem elementary to you. It will remind you of what you already know—the basics of the gospel. So why should you read this chapter? Because everyone can use

**87**

a refresher course now and then. You must be confident in your knowledge of the gospel you are sharing if you want to do so clearly and effectively.

# All Have Sinned

*10–1.  How would you summarize Romans 1–3?*

According to these chapters, all humanity is sinful when compared to God's holiness and is without excuse in needing a Savior. The Jews had the Law, yet they were disobedient. The Gentiles, though not possessing the written law of God, also sinned against His holy standards.

*10–2.  Have you met someone who tried to prove he or she was a good person? To what "good" actions did he or she point?*

Some people foolishly think they are good enough to enter heaven. Others do realize their need of God—or at least some kind of Supreme Being or Force—and try various ways to attain a right standing with Him—or It. They may seek cosmic approval by adopting a set of religious or moral rules and striving to live by those rules. But according to Romans 3:20, no set of rules, not even the Old Testament law, can make a person righteous, because no one can keep the rules perfectly. For this reason, God has provided sinners with righteousness through Christ (verse 21).

**10–3.** *How would you explain to someone trying to use a system of moral and social rules to gain God's favor that his or her plan will not work?*

The righteousness God offers is based on faith in Jesus Christ rather than in a person's ability to keep the Law (verse 22). Even before He established the Law, God knew it would never save anyone. Not a single person has the self-control to keep every command in the Law without making at least one mistake. Why did God bother to institute it? Because the Law pointed people to God's ultimate plan for salvation—a new covenant with believers based on His righteousness through Christ.

God's righteousness through Christ is available to all. In fact, all need it. When it comes to sin, there is no distinction between Jew and Gentile or any other human classification. Verse 23 clearly states that "all have sinned," or missed the mark, in trying to attain the holiness required by God.

**10–4.** *If you were witnessing to someone and he or she claimed to be innocent of sin because he or she had not murdered or stolen, how could you help this person to see that even the "small" sins are enough to make us miss God's mark?*

It might help when witnessing to offer that person a one-sentence summary of human history: We were created by a holy and righteous God to be holy, but we sinned and so fell "short of the glory of God." Even the smallest sin in human eyes is an ugly blemish compared to the sinless nature of God. This is why people—all people—need a Savior.

Romans 5:6–8 also indicates humanity's sinfulness. Before accepting Christ, a person is "powerless" to do anything that could save him or her. Thankfully, Christ did not wait until anyone was deserving of His sacrifice before He made it.

**10–5.** *What do you think is the best way to tell a person he or she is "powerless" to overcome sin without your coming across as arrogant or condemning?*

10–6. *How could you use Romans 5:6–8 to explain the dilemma of sinners and God's love for them?*

# All Must Confess

When the people to whom you are witnessing recognize their sinfulness, show them how to gain God's forgiveness for their sins through Jesus. Romans 10:9–13 presents the twin essentials for salvation—confession and belief. To be saved one must "confess with [his or her] mouth, 'Jesus is Lord.'" This confession, in turn, must be based on believing "God raised him from the dead."

10–7. *Why is it vital that a person believe in Christ's deity and His resurrection from the dead to be saved?*

Many people believe in Jesus as a great prophet or ethical teacher, but such belief is not enough. He is either everything

He said He was or a fraud. Jesus' resurrection proved He is who He claimed to be (1:4). It is only because He is divine that His death could do anything to deal with a person's sins and bring him or her into right standing with God.

*10–8. Why do you think God made confession of one's beliefs about Jesus necessary for salvation?*

# Saved By Grace

When the person you are witnessing to understands both his or her sinfulness and the salvation God made possible through Jesus Christ, reemphasize that salvation is a gift. Many times, people back away from becoming a Christian because they still have a lingering doubt that they do not deserve to be saved. But Scripture is clear: salvation is by God's grace alone and is utterly unearned (Ephesians 2:8,9).

*10–9. Why do you think it is so difficult for many people to accept a salvation they did not work to get?*

According to Romans 3:24, the person you are witnessing to can be "justified freely" by God's grace. The word *justify* is a legal term that means "to declare righteous." Righteousness is not earned, but given to believers. Jesus accomplished this by being the "sacrifice of atonement" for sin (verse 25).

*10–10. What do you think the prospect of being declared righteous before God would mean to an unwed mother? an alcoholic? one of your coworkers? one of your neighbors?*

# Chapter Review

The theology of salvation is very complex and is the cause for much debate and discussion among biblical scholars. But you do not have to understand the intricacies of why God's plan for salvation works. If you understand the basics of the gospel that have been revealed in this chapter, you are well prepared to give a clear explanation of the need for salvation and the way to it.

*10–11. In one sentence, write an explanation of the gospel you would feel comfortable using to witness to a person.*

Look around you; there are any number of people with whom you have at least minimal contact on a daily, weekly, or possibly occasional basis. This pool of people is a wonderful place in which to start sharing your faith. Almost always start with your testimony, but do not leave out a clear, concise explanation of the gospel, such as the one you recorded on the previous page.

Above all, pray for the people to whom God will lead you to witness. Ask that He will have prepared their hearts and already begun convicting them of their need for Him before you share the gospel. Then prepare yourself to do it.

**10-12. List five unsaved people for whom you will start praying that they be prepared to listen to the gospel and that you will be given opportunity to witness to them.**

- 

- 

- 

- 

-

You must be sensitive and obedient to the Holy Spirit in witnessing.

11

# Being A Ready Witness

You remember the words from your childhood: "On your mark. Get set. Go!" You probably yelled them as one long phrase. Written out, you can see three distinct instructions. Regardless of her speed, if a runner does not have her fingers planted at the line and her feet set firm against the staggered blocks, she will not be ready when the gun goes off and the other runners start.

The same is true of believers and witnessing. If you picture sharing the gospel as a race, you can easily see the importance of being ready to witness whenever the opportunity appears. What can you do to prepare yourself to explain the gospel at a moment's notice? This chapter will help you find out what it takes to be on your mark and set to go.

## Being Led By The Spirit

Just as every runner has an assigned lane in which she must run, you have the promptings of the Holy Spirit to keep you on track when sharing your faith. If you follow the Spirit's lead, your witnessing efforts will maintain a straight course.

Philip, an early believer, ran after the Spirit in sharing his precious faith. Already, the people of Samaria had experienced a great revival with Philip as the evangelist (Acts 8:5–25). But the Spirit needed him to be ready for another race. In verse 26, an angel appeared to Philip and told him to leave Samaria and head toward Gaza, a town about 60 miles south of Jerusalem. Philip might have thought he was going to minister in Gaza as he had in Samaria and put off leaving until the next day. But he did not. Instead, he obeyed immediately.

**11–1.** *What might have happened if Philip had not been ready to obey immediately? How does this illustrate the necessity for you to be sensitive to the Spirit and ready to act?*

You may not always understand what God is doing or why He is doing it. God's ways and thoughts are higher than yours (Isaiah 55:9). You do not have to understand exactly what is going on before you heed the Spirit's leading.

**11–2.** *Have you ever obeyed the Spirit's prompting to witness when you did not understand why you were being led to that particular person? What was the outcome?*

In Philip's case, God had a rendezvous set up between the evangelist and an Ethiopian official seeking full knowledge of God's truth (Acts 8:27,28). This man was probably a convert to Judaism returning home from worshiping in Jerusalem. And at the Spirit's prompting, Philip was ready to introduce that man to Jesus Christ (verse 29).

God was able to use Philip to witness to the Ethiopian because Philip was willing to obey the Spirit, even if it meant leaving a great crusade and going into the desert. In much the same way, God can use you to witness to people when you are sensitive and obedient to the Holy Spirit. He will bring you in contact with those who are ready to respond to the gospel.

11–3. *When you have prayed lately, to whom have you felt the Spirit prompting you to witness? What instructions has the Spirit given you about sharing the gospel with this person?*

# Being Ready To Answer

As Philip approached the chariot, he heard the eunuch reading from Isaiah. Immediately, Philip asked the man if he understood what he was reading (Acts 8:30,31). Philip used the man's spiritual condition and interests as a basis for telling him about Jesus.

If you listen to those around you, their conversations often reveal their spiritual needs. If you are alert and sensitive to these people, God can provide opportunities for you to lead them from their present spiritual condition to a relationship with Christ.

**11–4.** *Think of the last unsaved person with whom you talked. What did he or she say that might give you a hint about the best way to approach him or her with the gospel?*

The eunuch was reading Isaiah 53:7,8, but he did not know about whom Isaiah was prophesying. Philip, sensitive to the Spirit, knew he had been led to this man to explain to him about Jesus Christ (Acts 8:32–35).

Not everyone you share the gospel with will be a person you know well. But if you look for what God is doing in any person's life and listen to what the Spirit is saying to you about that person, you will recognize the way to share the gospel that will have the most meaning for him or her.

**11–5.** *God often leads you to people He has been preparing to receive the gospel. What are some of the ways He might be preparing the person He keeps reminding you about?*

# Making Jesus Known

Philip took the Isaiah passage to its logical end—Jesus Christ, the prophesied Messiah (Acts 8:35). As far as we know, Philip did not have a memorized presentation of the gospel. But he was so familiar with God's Word and the gospel that he was able to give the eunuch a brief but very rich lesson on becoming a follower of Jesus Christ.

It is good to memorize a series of Bible verses, such as "The Roman Road," that can help to lead a person to Christ. But if you will also spend time each day reading and studying God's Word, you will be even better prepared to witness in any situation.

11–6.  *How important do you think being equipped with knowledge about your faith and the Bible is to successfully following the Spirit's leading to witness? Why do you think this?*

11–7.  *What can you do this week to increase your understanding of Bible passages that would help you lead a person to Christ?*

The eunuch responded immediately to Philip's message, asking if he could be baptized. Philip had evidently explained to this man the need to be baptized in water. (See Matthew 28:19,20; Acts 8:36.) Then Philip took him down into the water and baptized him (verse 38).

11–8. *Do you think this account promises that every person to whom you witness will respond as the Ethiopian eunuch did? Why or why not?*

According to verses 39 and 40, after Philip baptized the eunuch, something supernatural happened. The Spirit of the Lord transported Philip to Azotus, never to see the eunuch again. The Ethiopian, however, returned home rejoicing after his divine meeting with Philip.

11–9. *What does the encounter between Philip and the eunuch tell you about the importance of seizing the moment when God brings you in contact with someone who is lost?*

God can use you to witness to others if you will prepare you heart and mind. If you will be open to the opportunities to witness that God brings to you, you will be amazed how often you will have opportunity to tell someone about Jesus.

While your personal testimony is good and proper for use in witnessing, you need to remember that you must also share God's Word. Only God's Word can produce the faith that is needed to accept Christ as Savior (Romans 10:17).

*11-10. Write a paragraph summarizing your salvation testimony, including how God has helped you to change now that you are a Christian. Within your testimony, quote two or three Bible verses that help explain what happened when you accepted Christ.*

# Chapter Review

True witnessing begins and ends with the Spirit of God. He knows the hearts of people and knows exactly what to do to reach them. He also knows exactly when they are open to receive the truth and will prepare them for the message. But you cannot overlook your part in the process. You need to be available for the Holy Spirit to use in witnessing to those whom He has prepared.

To be equipped to witness, prepare your heart through prayer. Ask God to help you be sensitive to the Holy Spirit and the needs of others. Let Him help you understand how you can use the needs of others as an avenue to share the gospel with them. Then keep your heart open as the Holy Spirit urges you to witness to those He brings your way.

You must also prepare your mind through the study of God's Word. Memorize those verses that explain God's plan of salvation. But more than that, spend time each day in God's Word. As you gain a greater grasp of the truths of the Word, you will be better equipped to witness in a variety of situations.

Remember, God wants you to be a witness. He has given the Holy Spirit to empower believers. If you have not been baptized in the Holy Spirit, ask Jesus to fill you. The Spirit will give you the power you need to witness.

**You must seize opportunities to witness to family and friends.**

# Reaching Family And Friends

A timid believer had been trying to witness to her cousin for years. At almost every family reunion and holiday, she managed to bring up her relationship with Jesus and how much it meant to her. Finally, the cousin asked, "You've been telling me how wonderful Jesus is for years. When are you going to introduce us?" The believer blushed; she had been so worried about not offending her cousin that she had failed to ever give her a clear gospel presentation.

Witnessing to your family members and longtime friends can be a tricky endeavor. You do not want to offend a loved one so much he or she refuses to talk to you. Yet you feel you must risk rejection by people you love in order to share the gospel which can save them from eternal torment.

This chapter addresses the thorny issue of reaching family and friends. There are no guarantees they will respond to a gospel presented with tact and love. You may do everything right, with plenty of sensitivity, yet still have a relative or friend reject the gospel and possibly you along with it. What this chapter can do is encourage you to take the risks to try to save the people you love.

# Winning Your Family

Witnessing to your family can be one of the most effective areas in which people can be won to the Lord. Since your family already knows you, you do not need to build a new relationship with them. Besides, they can readily observe the changes Christ makes in your life. These changes may be the very thing that draws them to Christ.

Simon and his brother Andrew had a fishing business on the Sea of Galilee. Evidently desiring to serve their God wholeheartedly, they left their business for a while to travel to Judea and listen to the teachings of a wild prophet named John the Baptist. According to John 1:35–42, Andrew and John (a fellow fisherman from the same town) were with John the Baptist one day when he saw Jesus and proclaimed Him as the Lamb of God. Andrew and John immediately followed Jesus and spent the evening talking with Him.

It was a transforming evening for Andrew: he became completely convinced that Jesus was none other than the promised Messiah. Excited about his incredible discovery, Andrew could think of no one he wanted to tell about Jesus more than his brother. Simon, evidently convinced of Andrew's sincerity and reliability, agreed to meet Jesus. This meeting changed Simon's life forever (verse 42).

12–1. *Andrew and Simon had been seeking spiritual truth. Do you think this made it easier for Simon to believe that Andrew might have really found the Messiah? Why or why not?*

12–2. *What unsaved members of your family have been searching for spiritual truth? How might this open the door for you to witness to them?*

Another thing that you can learn from Andrew is his unabashed enthusiasm for his message. You will only witness to your family members if you are thrilled about Jesus. If your faith is lackluster, you will find it easy to make up excuses for not sharing that faith with them. But if you cannot imagine anyone not wanting to have the relationship with Christ that you do, then you will find it easy to push past any excuses and introduce your loved ones to Jesus. It takes courage, but you will do it easily enough if you are excited about Christ.

12–3. *Do you think Andrew's excitement in telling his brother about Jesus was purely emotional or something deeper? Why or why not?*

*12–4.* *How has your enthusiasm for Jesus, or lack of it, influenced the frequency and effectiveness of your witnessing to unsaved relatives?*

Think about the church leader Simon Peter later became. When discouraged in witnessing to a relative, imagine what he or she might be with the Lord living in him or her. Then pray for wisdom and boldness to proclaim the gospel.

# Telling A Friend

The day after Jesus had called Peter to be His disciple, He found Philip and commanded him: "Follow me" (John 1:43). Since Philip, Peter, and Andrew were from the same town, they possibly knew each other. Perhaps it was easy for Philip to follow Jesus because Peter and Andrew had already made that commitment (verse 44).

*12–5.* *What unsaved, casual friends do you have with whom you have something in common? How could you use shared experiences to witness to them?*

Also convinced Jesus was the Messiah, Philip searched out a friend of his own, Nathanael, and told him he had found the One prophesied by Moses. The Messiah was none other than "Jesus of Nazareth, the son of Joseph" (verse 45).

**12–6.** *Name a close friend—possibly one you grew up with or have worked with for some time—who needs to meet Jesus. How could you share Christ with him or her in a relevant way?*

Notice how Philip handled Nathanael's skepticism. As a friend, he could have felt free to argue the point. Instead, Philip invited Nathanael to see for himself what Jesus was like and make his own decision (verse 46). The Lord has not called you to force the gospel on anyone, but He has called you to point your friends to Him.

**12–7.** *Have you ever tried to argue a friend into believing the gospel because you wanted so badly for that friend to know Jesus? What was the end result?*

Imagine if Philip had responded: "That's just like you, Nate! Always the skeptic!" Thankfully, Philip reacted with tact, something vital when witnessing to your friends. If you extend the same courtesy to a friend that you would extend to a stranger, you will have a much better chance of seeing that friend accept Christ (verses 47–49).

*12–8. **What are some tactful responses you might give to a friend who is initially resistant to your sharing the gospel?***

Incidentally, Nathanael's doubt was not a rejection of Philip or of Jesus, but an honest question from someone who simply wanted to know the truth. You may know your friends well, but the Holy Spirit knows them infinitely better. Allow Him to lead you in effectively witnessing to both your casual and close friends who need to meet Jesus Christ.

## Leaving A Faith Legacy

If you have not already reached this point in your life, you will someday find yourself at the mature end of many of your relationships with friends and family—parent, grandparent, mentor. If anything, it is even more vital at this stage in life that you continue reaching out to unsaved relatives and friends. Why? Because you will be establishing your legacy. And as a believer, you want that legacy to say a great deal about the need for Christ.

*12–9. How have you spiritually benefited from the example of an older, Christian friend or relative? How does this influence the kind of legacy you want to pass on to others?*

Timothy became a leader in the Christian community because of the influence of several older believers. Although Paul and Timothy were not relatives, Paul treated Timothy as if he were his son (2 Timothy 1:1,2). Through many years of side-by-side ministry, the apostle had poured himself into Timothy, discipling and training him with his experience and wisdom.

*12–10. If you were to die today, would you be remembered by your friends for your personality or for your devotion to the Lord and how you made Him real to them? How do you feel about your answer?*

Paul, however, was not the first to teach God's Word to Timothy. He had a godly grandmother and mother, Lois and Eunice, who had instilled their faith in him (verse 5).

*12–11. What kind of legacy are you leaving your family members, including children, nieces, nephews, and other relatives? Do they look up to you for your undivided devotion to the Lord?*

# Chapter Review

Crusades, television programs, and street evangelism have each reached many people with the gospel. But by far the most effective way to witness is for believers like you to share your faith with your friends and relatives. What makes this method of evangelism so effective? People for whom you care and with whom you have developed relationships are more inclined to listen to what you have to say than are complete strangers. As they see God changing you, they will know He can do the same for them.

The exciting thing about reaching your friends and family with the gospel is that each one reached has his or her own network of friends and relatives to witness to. The more that you and others witness to those you know, the greater the potential harvest.

Make a list of your unsaved family members and friends. Begin to pray for them to be saved. Ask God to show you ways you can effectively share the gospel with them. Then begin to look for opportunities to tell them about Jesus.

**Notes**

# Notes